Hidden Pearls

Lendia Sherman

Relentless Publishing House, LLC
Columbia, SC

RELENTLESS
PUBLISHING

Hidden Pearls

© 2019 by Lendia Sherman.

Published by:
Relentless Publishing House, LLC

ISBN: 978-1-948829-90-8

First Edition: October 2019

DEDICATION

This book is dedicated to all young ladies seeking to belong and find their purpose…you are not forgotten.

A Mother's Love

TABLE OF CONTENTS

Sharing

Here I stand, wondering how to make it. No one alive could understand what I was going through, but I stumbled upon a little voice:

"And they overcame Him by the words of their testimony, and by the Blood of the Lamb"

Revelation 12:11

Big problems, little problems, they are all the same. However, knowing that there is someone who can give you peace will determine how large the problem will or will not get. This book was written in hopes of opening the eyes of every woman who reads and shares her testimony as God has commanded us to do. Sharing your story at the God-given time may help inspire someone in need.

This book is intended to inspire all ladies, young or old to their DESTINY.

Chapter One

Outer Body

Hi! My name is Mary. I am ten years old. One cool fall day in November around 5:30 p.m. it all started. Guess what, I entered into this place we call a loving world, weighing eight pounds and four ounces. I was twenty-two inches long. WOW! What a bundle of joy! I had a beautiful, full head of black hair with lots of curls and a tiny smile that accentuated my face just right, so I heard. My mother held me with such love! Tears fell from her eyes onto my cheeks. My father, a tall, dark and handsome young man looked as if he would eat me alive. He stood over me with disbelief as great big tears fell from his eyes. They were big enough for ducks to wade in. Yet they were the tears of joy and love. They took me home and placed me in a big bright yellow room with piles of bears, both of which by the way became my favorite color and animal. For eleven months I would hear the big golden bear singing as I fell asleep and singing as I awoke each morning.

I was greeted on my first birthday by my mother, father and the big pot-bellied bear that I loved so much. My mother stood there, with her long hair cascading down her shoulders, clapping in unison with my dad, who was dressed in all black. He reminded me of a supreme court judge. Their rendition of Happy Birthday made me squeal with delight and a bit of fright. What a scene! What a way to be awakened! There stood the people and bear that I loved the most hovering over me, singing at the top of their lungs. My daddy picked me up in an effort to calm me down. How great it felt to be in his arms as he held me as tight as he could. On second thought, I might have been holding him as tight as I could. That day was the first of many more to come like that.

Each new year brought a new, furry friend. My second year brought a fluffy, orange, striped tiger. Year three came the big grey donkey with floppy ears. Year four I was joined by my little pink pig. By year five there were no more fluffy animals, but rather a very special girl who spoke Spanish. By year ten, the new friends disappeared altogether. Nevertheless, my mother kept all of my birthday pictures. That was all and well, because in that year life would become different. This is where my dream became a nightmare.

My hero was gone!

One cool and foggy morning in late October, my daddy started out for work. As he hurried toward the door, he stretched out his long arms, grabbed my fluffy cheeks and gave me a great big wet kiss. This was nothing new; daddy always gave me a kiss before he left for work. Daddy said I will always be his little baby, even at the age of ten. He also enjoyed kissing mommy too! With a big smile on his face, he said, "I'll see you at the carnival tonight." WOW, I almost forgot the carnival was tonight! What a festive time of the year. There would be loads of balloons, cake-walks, apple bobbing, fishing games and treasure hunts. The treasure hunt was my favorite. I enjoyed the hayrides, never knowing where the driver was going to take us was exciting in itself. Feeling the wind blowing through my hair as we traveled through the hills was lots of fun too. After returning from our exciting trip, we were treated to a giant cup of hot chocolate with whipped cream on top. I would immediately make a whipped cream mustache, and my daddy would gently clean my face after reaching into his pocket for his white handkerchief.

Anyway let me stop day dreaming,
and tell you my story.

Mommy and I went about our daily routine. I was dropped off early for school, and mommy hurried off to work. My mind would not stop thinking about the carnival. I think my whole class was excited about the fall carnival. Despite the excitement that my fourth grade classmates and I had, Ms. Thompson, our teacher, went on with our studies as usual. She would call on a student to answer a question, but their little mind would be on the carnival. We were only focused on the things we were going to do at the fall carnival. No one could stay focus on school work.

Finally, after lunch, Ms. Thompson let our class finish decorating the classroom for the night's festivities. Our classroom would be used for the apple bobbing games. We had apples hanging for the ceiling and paper trees surrounding the room. Our room really looked like an apple orchard. My friend Ashley and I talked about where we would meet and the games we would play first. The bell finally rang. We were all excited to see our parents. Mom picked me up. Then we picked up the cakes that would be used for the cake-walk. In addition, we picked up extra bags of apples. We stopped at my favorite restaurant, the one with the big arches, and had a quick dinner. I could barely eat, the excitement of meeting my friend Ashley was overwhelming! It was 4:30 in the afternoon when I spoke with daddy on the phone. He was just as excited as me and mom. Mommy finished all of her errands and we headed for the carnival.

We finally arrived and dropped off all the goodies mom and I had picked up. It was time for the carnival and there was no sign of dad. "He's going to meet us after he finishes with work. It's probably taking longer than he thought it would," mom said. I saw my best friend Ashley and her mother. We waved one another down. Running towards each other, we greeted each other with a big smile and huge hug. Mrs. Jones and mom talked as Ashley and I dragged them around from game to game. In spite of mom speaking to dad earlier, she began to look a little worried when I asked about him. Again, she pulled out her phone to call him, but still no answer. She even tried calling him at home, hoping he went by the house first, but there was no answer there either. After Ashley and I played Pin-the-Tale-on-the-Donkey and only winning six pieces of candy we got a little tired. Mrs. Jones and mom had talked for several hours while we played lots of games at the carnival, but I wanted to see my dad. Besides, I always rode the hayride with dad, and it was getting close to closing time. Mom said, "Since it is getting late we should take the ride with Mrs. Jones and Ashley".

Maybe dad just couldn't get away. Sometimes he had to work really late. We all agreed. After the hayride, mom and I stayed a while visiting with other friends and playing games. The night had gone and still no dad. My heart was a little sad.

Journey home

We started our journey home. I began to drift off to sleep. As we got closer to our home I heard mom say, "What is going on!" I opened my eyes to flashing blue and red lights. I could hear the police cars' sirens. As we neared our house, we realized that the lights were in fact at our house! I asked my mother, "What's happening? Why are they at our house? Is there a fire at our house? Did someone break in? What's going on?" Her only answer was, "Shh!! I don't know! Shh!!! Shh! Be quiet! Let's see what's going on." As we pulled into the driveway, the police officer, Deputy Smith, asked mommy if we lived here and if she had any type of identification on her. Mom responded with a nervous yes and pulled out her driver's license. He then asked her to step out of the car. They walked to the back of the car. I saw Deputy Smith grab mommy's hand and tell her something. Mommy fell to the ground as Deputy Smith tried desperately to hold her up. I jumped out of the car, screaming as loud as I could, "What's wrong with my mommy?" When I got to the back of the car mommy grabbed me and told me that dad had been in a serious car accident. I began to ask questions, " Is he okay? Is he in the house? Is he at the hospital? Where is my daddy? I screamed!" With tears running down her cheeks, mom said, "He had passed away. He died about an hour ago." As the words fell from her lips, I lost consciousness. When I came to, I was in my bed thinking it had all been a bad nightmare . I looked around my room, no daddy, but lots of people standing over me. The only words I could understand were those of Deputy Smith saying, "It will be alright."

I could hear my mother repeating what Deputy Smith had told her, "I am very sorry Mrs. Williams. There has been a serious accident. Around 7:30 p.m., your husband's vehicle was hit by a fuel tanker which lost control on Highway 39. The tanker burst into flames and your husband's vehicle burst into flames on impact. I'm sorry, Mrs. Williams to be the one to inform you of this tragedy, but your husband did not survive." She made an awful groaning sound as she told the horrific story to our family and friends over and over again. I don't know if it was my father's death or my mother's scream that drove me into a state of shock. I don't know how long my mind had been living outside of my body.

Outer body experience

For days it felt like I was living in someone else's body. I don't remember getting dressed. I don't remember eating. I don't remember having anything to drink. I don't remember taking a bath. The morning of the funeral I came to myself. I saw this long box in front of me. I was wearing a black laced dress, black tights and a warm black sweater. Many people walked around giving my mother their condolences. Not one thing seemed to matter. I was still having an outer body experience.

Everything about my daddy kept running through my head. It was as if I was watching a movie, but at the end of the movie, he was gone. No one could say or do anything to take that awful pain away. Day after day, tears would just flow like a raging river from my tiny brown eyes. Then other days I would be in a trance. I would frequently have an outer body experience.

Finally, after days of visitors, the crowd had dissipated. I stood in my bedroom window watching the last car drive away. It was still and quiet in our home. All of a sudden I felt two warm loving arms wrap around me, yet squeezing me so gently. A small quiet voice began to whisper in my ear, "*I love you, and your father loved you too.*" With tears streaming down her face my mother and I found comfort in each other. She softly whispered stories of daddy spending time with us, reminding me how he would give us a kiss before he would leave for work, read a bedtime story to me before I fell asleep in his arms, and how he and I would have our own little pizza party when he sometimes got off early from work. Most of all, she reminded me that daddy believed in God, and knowing that daddy knew God gave us inner peace.

Memories

Several weeks passed. My mother and I made scrapbooks to help keep the fond memories in our hearts. Mom wanted to be able to tell my children, her grandchildren, about their grandfather. So now I can keep all the great memories of my dad around. Sometimes I have sad days but I go back to my memory bank and pull up all the great things such as making a mustache with the cool whip from our hot chocolate, having a camping trip in the backyard and other things that my dad would say and do for my mom and I. My birthday and or the fall carnival have never been the same. I can no longer see that tall, dark giant standing over my bed singing Happy Birthday. However, I do take peace in knowing that my daddy knew God. So always remember that knowing God will help you through the challenges you may face. I pray that my story will comfort you in your troubled times.

Know that there is a blessing in every story.

Daddy taught me about God, so I believe that my daddy is with God in Heaven. Every once in a while I look toward Heaven and say "Hello daddy, I love and miss you!"

"And they overcame him (Satan) by the words of their testimony, and by the Blood of the Lamb…"

Revelation 12:11

Chapter Two

He Touched Me

I just have to tell someone. I can't keep this inside anymore. Hi, my name is Brenda. I am 15 years old. I have long sandy, red hair, which stops in the middle of my back. My long brown legs are perfect for running track or walking down the runway, but I have a problem. I have large breast for a girl of my size. I am a 36 F and this is not good for a teenager who's a size 4! I have two stepbrothers, James and Venus, and one stepsister named Marie. My stepfather, James Sr. has two other children, a daughter named Mary and a son named Tommy. Neither has the same mother. What a perfect family. I used to be very outgoing, always looking for someone to give me that perfect love.

What is perfect Love?

God is Love!

My mother would always tell me how God loved me. She is a great mother. To me she is a walking image of God's pure love, always making sacrifices to ensure we have everything we needed. She worked several jobs to provide for our family. I loved the second job. She worked at a seafood restaurant. When we were low on food she would bring home the best dinners. She would always say that God will provide. God will always give is best. He gave the greatest sacrifice, His Beloved Son, so that all men might have eternal life. My stepfather knew of God, but didn't live like he knew Him. Talk about being a hypocrite and being unequally yoked! That's the photo of my parents.

As you might have guessed my stepfather had to take care of his extended family as well as his immediate family. He had lots of extracurricular activities to manage (if you know what I mean). We were not poor by any means, or at least that's what I thought. My mother tried to make us feel as if we were well off. It even appeared as if my sibling and I had the best life any child could ever ask for. However, living in a shotgun house tells a story of its own.

Then one day in a matter of minutes, my life changed drastically. I decided to relax by lounging around the house and studying for a history exam. I hated memorizing names and dates. I didn't believe that history will play a major role later in my life, so it became a challenge for me to overcome. My stepfather was at home as well. He too had decided to catch up on his rest.

What a coincident.

After studying for what seemed like hours, I left my room to get a drink of water. My stepfather was in the kitchen. He gave me a weird look as I reached for a glass from the cabinet. All of a sudden, a cold chill went down my spine. I could hear a little voice telling me to go back to my room, but I ignored it.

God speaks to us in many different ways to help

*guide and protect us. Pay attention to that quiet
little voice that speaks to your inner man.*

When I turned toward the refrigerator, my stepfather grabbed my breast. Yes, my stepfather. Immediately, I tried to push his hand away, but it was as if I was pushing a brick wall. I couldn't scream. I was frozen stiff. My mouth was open, but not a sound escaped. He then pushed me against the refrigerator. My step–father is about six feet seven inches tall and weighs over 240 pounds. I only weigh 105 pounds. He pulled my shirt up. I tried to fight back, but again, I was no match for him. I felt his hand move under my shirt, under my bra and grabbed my breast. I thought I would pass out, I tried to fight back. He had undressed me from the waist down before my mind could completely comprehend what was happening!

Introduction to Sex

This was my introduction to sex. Yes, sex, by a person who was supposed to protect me. He proceeded to penetrate me. Yes, my step–father. I stood there, tears running down my face, wanting to pass out, but I knew I had to be strong and try to fight for myself. The pain was indescribable. Although, it only took him three or four minutes, it felt like hours. When he had finished with me, he looked at me in disgust and told me to go and get cleaned up and get out of his sight. As I started to run out of the kitchen, he grabbed me by my hair and told me if I told anyone he would kill me and my mother. Being that he was very intimidating and I was very afraid of him, I believed every word that came out of his mouth. He was very abusive and had serious anger issues. He beat my mother on several occasions, causing her bodily injuries. On one occasion, he broke her arm, and she told everyone she fell. On another occasion he blackened both of her eyes.

An overwhelming fear came over me, as tears continued to run down my face. In contrast, my mother had spoken to me on many occasions about sex and when it would be appropriate. The "Not until you are married speech".

God has someone special for you.
Keep yourself clean and pure.

Even if I can't see you, God can see you.

But what she told me was totally different from what I experienced that day. My mother is a Christian. She would always remind us to pray and study the Bible. She kept me and my siblings in the church and around people who proclaim Christ as their Savior. My mother would come into our rooms at night and pray for us. But on this day I recalled Tamar in the Bible.

2 Samuel 13: 1-15 (KJV)

1. *And it came to pass after this, that Absalom the son of David had a fair sister, whose name was Tamar and Amnon the son of David, loved her.*
2. *And Amnon was so vexed, that he fell sick for his sister Tamar; for she was a virgin; and Amnon thought it hard for him to do anything to her.*

3. *But Amnon had a friend, whose name was Jonadab, the son of Shimeah David's brother: and Jonadab was a very subtle man.*

4. *And he said unto him, Why art thou, being the king's son, lean from day to day? wilt thou not tell me? And Amnon said unto him, I love Tamar my brother Absalom's sister.*

5. *And Jonadab said unto him, Lay thee down on thy bed, and make thyself sick: and when thy father cometh to see thee, say unto him, I pray thee, Let my sister Tamar come, and give me meat, and dress the meat in my sight, that I may see it, and eat it at her hand.*

6. *So Amnon lay down, and made himself sick: and when the king was come to see him, Amnon said unto the king, I pray thee, let Tamar my sister come, and make me a couple of cakes in my sight, that I may eat at her hand.*

7. *Then David sent home to Tamar saying, Go now to thy brother Amnon's house, and dress him meat. So Tamar went to her*

brother Amnon's house: and he was laid down. And she took flour, and kneaded it, and made cakes in his sight, and did bake the cakes.

8. And she took a pan, and poured them out before him: but he refused to eat. And Amnon said, have out all men from me. And they went out every man from him.

9. And Amnon said unto Tamar, Bring the meat into the chamber, that I may eat of thine hand. And Tamar took the cakes which she had made, and brought them into the chamber to Amnon her brother.

11. And when she had brought them unto him to eat, he took hold of her, and said unto her, Come lie with me, my sister.

12. And she answered him, Nay, my brother, do not force me; for no such thing ought to be done in Israel: do not thou this folly.

13. And I, wither shall I cause my shame to go? And as for thee, thou shalt be as one of the fools in Israel. Now therefore, I pray thee, speak unto the king; for he will not withhold me from thee.

14. *Howbeit he would not hearken unto her voice: but, being stronger that she, forced her, and lay with her.*

15. *Then Amnon hated her exceedingly; so that the hatred wherewith he hated her was greater that the love wherewith he had loved her. And Amnon said unto her, Arise, be gone.*

After staying in the bathroom for what seemed to be an eternity trying to wash his smell off of me, my body felt numb. Yet, my body continued to throb. Every part of my body seemed to hurt. It hurt so much that I know longer knew where the pain was coming from. I wanted to climb out of the bathroom window, but I was too afraid. I wanted to scream, but I was too afraid. How I prayed someone would come home.

Then, I heard my brother come in the house. I left the bathroom, but to my surprise my stepfather had left the house. As I laid in my bed in the fetal position, I questioned why God had punished me in such an awful way. No clear answer came. I became withdrawn, believing I had caused this to happen. I could not tell anyone. I began to hate men. I prayed that God would kill all men. Seeing that God didn't want to kill them, I decided to take matters into my own hands. I became very promiscuous. I decided to have sex with every male I could. Maybe, just maybe, I would get some dreadful disease and kill them all. Then I would have the last laugh. I even took money from some of them. I didn't care how old they were. I tried to have sex with all of my stepfather's friends. Men, they were all the same. My stepbrothers were so much like their father; they forced themselves on me too.

Signs

I wanted to hurt him the way he hurt me. I should have known, by the way he beat my mother that he hated me too.

The atmosphere in our house had changed. It would go from the happy, smiling, loud laughter of teenage children to afraid to speak above a whisper teenage children. We did not know if we were going to get punched in the mouth for talking too loud or punched in the chest for running in the house. My mother would even be on pins and needles. My mother whispered when my stepfather was around. Again, he was so abusive toward my mother she would work two jobs just to get away. She always tried to work when she knew he would be at home, hoping that this would calm him down. She had no clue that he was abusing me. I didn't know how to tell her. This is stuff you only see on television, right. NOT! It happens here in Georgia too!

Sometimes my stepfather would take the family on trips to the beach, Six Flags, or even Disney World, to make up for his hideous behavior, especially after an abusive attack. After our encounter, I no longer wanted to go on family trips. I was terrified of his behavior, especially if he got drunk because he would turn into some type of demon. He would punch my stepbrothers until they would bleed from their noses. He would slap my mother until she would hang her head as the tears ran down her face, but for me a got the name calling; slut and liar to name a couple. He loved to call me ugly. Often my mother did have enough courage to fight for me verbally for me to stay with my aunts, my biological father's sisters, while they were away. However, they were lesbians, so I got involved with being with other women. Being I was a secret keeping, I was never able to tell my aunties. The more I tried to get out, the deeper I got in.

Drugs became my solution to every problem. Even though I prayed to God to help me, I still couldn't get out. I couldn't tell my mother because she was such a loving person. Yes, she felt something wasn't right. She would always ask me if something was wrong. With a big smile, "Oh, nothing, mom, all is well." All the while I was dying inside, looking for a way out! I continued to go to church, hoping for some type of sign or a prayer or two answered in order to get out of the hell I was living.

There is a God

One Tuesday night at the end of Bible Study,

my preacher asked if anyone needed prayer. Now I knew I needed prayer, but I was too afraid to go up in front of what seemed like at least a hundred finely dressed people looking as if they had no problems.

I had just turned sixteen years old and had sex with over twenty-five men and ten females. I had done the very thing that my mother had taught me not to do. I was a SINNER! I was on my way to Hell! But my pastor would say, "There's no sin too big for God to forgive." "Come, come now don't be ashamed. He then got specific. "If you have been in homosexual encounters, come." Come! How did he know these things about me? Yes, I had all these issues in my life, BUT if I went up in front of all those people, everyone would know. Shame kicked in. This would surely kill my mother. In this small town everyone would talk about my mother. I could not have that happen. My mother meant too much to me, but it seemed like my pastor wouldn't stop. He looked straight into my eyes. Inside I was dying. I wanted to cry but no tears fell. After the alter call, my pastor's wife, Mrs. Anderson, pulled me into her office. "Hello, daughter, you know God loves you and He wants to set you free". "You can still give it to Him baby, it is ok." As she finished her statement, my pastor, Pastor Anderson, came into her office. He said again, "God does answer prayers and He is here for you". I cried, "Yes Lord! Yes, take it away! Yes Lord! Yes Lord, here I am, take it all away!" I remember falling to the floor crying uncontrollably.

Then a peace, which I can't begin to describe, came over me. My pastor's wife wrapped her arms around me and began to speak life filled words to me such as, "You are Blessed, You are Beautiful, You are wonderful and fearfully made, yes, He created you for a purpose and you belong to God." She had scriptures already written down for me to study. The list was two pages long. What stuck out in my mind was how they knew all these things about me. After I got home that night, I read all the scriptures she had given me. I prayed for forgiveness for all my wrong doings and I even prayed for my stepfather. Something happened that night which provoked me to seek God every moment I was awake. I no longer wanted to hang out. I just wanted God. Mrs. Anderson would call and check on me daily. She said God had assigned her to help guide me in the right direction. I continued to pray for my family. My prayer would always consist of God giving my family a chance to repent of their sins.

In December 1980, my stepfather was admitted into the hospital because he had been diagnosed with liver cancer. I would often visit my stepfather in the hospital and pray for him. I asked him if he knew Christ as his Savior. He did not. He was able to except Christ as his Savior, but not before he apologized for the things he did to me. Two weeks later my stepfather passed away. Before he passed away he told my mother of the things he had done to me. She was really hurt and ashamed. My mother and I became best friends. She apologized for all the pain she caused me, for leaving me around my stepfather while she worked to stay away from him. My prayer is that everyone turns from their wicked and evil ways and give their life to a true and living God before He returns. Know that God does hear your cry. Just hold on. God will deliver you!

"And they overcame him (Satan) by the Blood of the and the words of their testimony…"

Revelation 12:11

Chapter Three

Reflection

O h, my God! What have I done? My children! I have destroyed their lives. I don't like what I see. I look at each of them and see myself. The things I have done. Why didn't I follow His Word?

What have I done?

The Bible tells us in Proverbs 22:6, "Train up a child in the way he should go: and when he is old, he will not depart from it."

BUT,

I didn't.

I, Genell Fleming, was only thinking about myself. Selfishness! I walked out, leaving my parents' home because I didn't want to follow the rules of the house. They were only trying to teach me how to be a self-respectful and respected person in society. A person who was a leader and not a follower. A person of great character and great standards. A person who would be able to contribute to society and make a great impact in the world. They were trying to teach me how to handle life according to their biblical beliefs.

Selfish, I had become. A rebel, I was. What a sad depiction I see when I look in the faces of my children. I chose self-gratification over nurturing my children. I put myself before them. The lust for the things of this world came before God and my children. I did this! I can't blame my choices on anyone except myself. No, this didn't come from my mother or father. They were the most loving parents any child could ask for. My only problem was I just didn't fit in. Little did I know, I wasn't supposed to fit in. I was chosen a long time ago by God for a special purpose.

Purpose

Did I know my purpose? Yes! I'm a songster. I love to sing, write songs, and music but I didn't want to commit to God or hard work. I wanted to be free to choose and so I did.

Mirror, Mirror, On the wall

I look at my now twenty-two year old daughter, my first born, dealing with rejection, hatred, anger and a lack of belonging.

Why!

I didn't know who her father was. Everything she is, I was. I chose to have fun with the boys. Having sex made me feel superior, in charge, so I used my body to manipulate men, but in that process I got caught.

D.N.A.

What you do in the dark will come to the light (an old wives tale, but true). I had a little girl named Courtney. Her daddy, James, took care of her for 5 years. He then changed his mind and no longer wanted to pay child support, so through the courts DNA tests were taken and James was not Courtney's father. I was ordered by the judge to bring in the names of the other guys I thought could be my baby's daddy so DNA test could be performed. We lucked up and found her father.

He now rejected Courtney, because he hated me for interrupting his life. He was a married man with a family of his own. Now the courts have ordered him to pay support for Courtney. His wife had no clue that her husband, the preacher, had been unfaithful to their family.

Anger

Courtney became very angry with life. At the age of 13 she became rebellious and sexually active. Anything that I would tell or ask her to do, she would do the opposite. Courtney do not have sex and she became sexually active. Courtney your curfew is at 9:00 P.M. and she would come home at 1:00 A.M. in the morning. Nothing I said could stop her. When I would speak to her about her behavior, she would just say, "You did it." The pain of disappointment and failure as a mother struck me deep within my soul; it became pretty overwhelming.

In the meantime my second child was born. Her name is Erica. Erica dealt with fear and rejection. The fear of the outburst and violence she'd seen.

The curse continued

I knew Erica's father, but I wasn't good enough for his family. So they rejected Erica and me. Here I am again dealing with a child that has been rejected by her father and his family. The cycle of rebellion continues.

Reflection

Here I am looking at that mirror again.

When will it stop?

I didn't know how to stand on my own. I began having babies at the age of sixteen. Now at thirty-eight years old I have four grandchildren. My babies are living the life I hated.

What have I done?

A continuous question in my mind!

Two young girls rejected, and their mother rejected, all looking for love. I had six different men living with us on six different occasions, two of which were married. I even allowed my girls to call them dad. I wanted them to have a father in the worst way. After number four, Courtney could no longer take it. She hated the fact that our house was a revolving door for men who were only after one thing: a place to lay their head free of charge. Courtney decided to try life for herself. She felt as if she needed to go her separate way.

Courtney got involved with a married man named Rodney, who would not take no for an answer, and became the father of her last child Ashley. After several beatings, Courtney wanted to call it quits, but that only infuriated Rodney. These beatings would leave her with a black eye, a broken wrist, and a fractured skull. Finally, she was able to escape from Rodney, however, he continued to stalk her for a while, then he laid back. No more Rodney. No more looking over her shoulders. No more hiding out. No more fear. The fear of being attacked had gone. She was no longer afraid to go out into the public. Courtney was finally on her way. She returned to school to receive her GED, and started college, majoring in Psychology to become a Social Worker. Courtney wanted to help women and children that had been exposed to the same life style she had been exposed too.

One Wednesday night after class, Rodney approached Courtney and tried to persuade her to return to him, but she refused. Rodney then pulled out a handgun and fired it twice, hitting her in the chest. He left the area leaving her for dead. Classmates and other bystanders call for help and stayed to help until help arrived.

Turning point!

Sitting in the emergency room holding hands with Erica, we prayed like we never prayed before.

God if you truly exist please come in and help us
now! Show us your hand of mercy and compassion!

As we came to the end of our prayer, we felt
an overwhelming sense of God's presence enter
the room. His restoring hands touched us all at the
same time. We wept with exceeding joy, a feeling
which is hard to fully explain. You had to have been
in the room to know the feeling. God healed
Courtney and she had a speedy recovery. He
healed our broken hearts. Once upon a time we
had a hunger to seek others for love, especially
men. We turned our focus toward each other,
ourselves and God. Courtney, returning home from
the hospital, started a recovery process for our
entire family. A lot of confessing and forgiving took
place. We no longer searched outside of God. We
set through Rodney's trial once he was captured
after being on the run for six months. Courtney
spoke on his behalf for the sentencing asking for
mercy on his sentence. Courtney had truly forgiven
Rodney for trying to kill her. She knew how to see
people for who they should really be and not what
they have become because of unwise choices.
She knew that sometimes people make bad

choices because of the lack of knowledge and love they have or did not have in their lives. Even though Courtney testified on behalf of Rodney, he still received twenty years for attempted murder. She really taught me something about forgiveness.

I was that prodigal child. I returned to my parents' home seeking and asking for forgiveness. They took me in as if I'd never left.

Prodigal son moment

Luke 15 11-32

11. *And He said, A certain man had twos sons:*

12. *And the younger of them said to his father, Father, give me the portion of goods that falleth to me. And he divided unto them his living.*

13. *And not many days after the younger son gathered all together, and took his journey into a far country, and there wasted his substance with riotous living.*

14. And when he had spent all, there arose a mighty famine in that land; and he began to be in want.

15. And he went and joined himself to a citizen of that country; and he sent him into his fields to feed swine.

16. And he would fain have filled his belly with the husks that the swine did eat: and no man gave unto him.

17. And when he came to himself, he said, How many hired servants of my father's have bread enough and to spare, and I perish with hunger!

18. I will arise and go to my father, and will say unto him, Father, I have sinned against heaven, and before thee.

19. And am no more worthy to be called thy son; make me as one of thy hired servants.

20. And he arose, and came to his father. But when he was yet a great way off, his father saw him, and had compassion, and ran, and fell on his neck, and kissed him.

21. *and the son said unto him, Father, I have sinned against heaven, and in thy sight, and am to more worthy to be called thy son.*

22. *But the father said to his servants, Bring forth the best robe, and put it on him; and put a ring on his hand, and shoes on his feet:*

23. *And bring hither the fatted calf, and kill it; and let us eat, and be merry:*

24. *For this my son was dead, and is alive again; he was lost, and is found. And they began to be merry.*

25. *Now his elder son was in the field: and as he came and drew near to the house, he heard music and dancing.*

26. *And he call one of the servants, and asked what these things meant.*

27. *And he said unto him, Thy brother is come; and thy father hath killed the fatted calf, because he hath received him safe and sound.*

28. *And he was angry, and would not go in: therefore came his father out, and entreated him.*

29. *And he answering said to his father, Lo, these many years do I serve thee, neither transgressed I at any time thy commandment: and yet thou never gavest me a kid, that I might make merry with my friends:*

30. *But as soon as this thy son was come, which hath devoured thy living with harlots, thou hast killed for him the fatted calf.*

31. *And he said unto him, Son, thou art ever with me, and all that I have is thine.*

32. *It was meet that we should make merry, and be glad; for this thy brother was dead, and is alive again; and was lost, and is found.*

We joined my parent's church and served under my father. From that day forward we began to pray against generational curses and that the enemy would no longer be able to have control over our lives.

The Bible works. We all are predestined for something. Keep searching until you find your purpose in life. Don't give up! Seek and you will find.

Remember you are loved!

"And they overcame him (Satan) by the words of their testimony, and by the Blood of the Lamb"

Revelation 12:11

ABOUT THE AUTHOR

L endia Sherman decided to Reboot after all her children left home by completing her Bachelor of Science in Psychology. She has collaborated with her daughters to open a business, DeStress, for ladies of all ages. She is an author of a children's book, "Pretty Little Me!" and co-author of a ReBoot journal. Lendia is a veteran of the United States Army. She is a mother and a grandmother. Lendia loves seeing ladies of all ages to reach their potential. Lendia Sherman was born and raised in Enterprise, Alabama, and currently reside in Augusta, Georgia.

www.ingramcontent.com/pod-product-compliance
Lightning Source LLC
Chambersburg PA
CBHW032103040426
42449CB00007B/1170